Gaetano Savatteri

Calò's Big Sprint

With a Foreword by
Andrea Camilleri

Translated from the Italian by
Warren Blumberg

Sellerio editore
Palermo

2008 © Sellerio editore via Siracusa 50 Palermo
e-mail: info@sellerio.it
www.sellerio.it

Savatteri, Gaetano <1964>

Calò's Big Sprint / Gaetano Savatteri ; with a Foreword by Andrea Ca-
milleri , translated from the Italian by Warren Blumberg. - Palermo :
Sellerio, 2008.
EAN 978-88-389-2370-8
I. Camilleri, Andrea <1925>   II. Blumberg, Warren
853.914 CDD-21

CIP – *Biblioteca centrale della Regione siciliana «Alberto Bombace»*

Originally published as *La volata di Calò*

A Race towards Freedom

by

Andrea Camilleri

Soon after the Allied landing in Sicily, which happened on the night of July 9th 1943, the German Hermann Goering division reached the line of defense that ran through Serradifalco. This was the town where many members of my family had taken refuge from the Allied bombing raids. Among those sheltered there were a grandfather, my two grandmothers, my mother, an aunt and an uncle. My father was in Porto Empedocle, where he was serving military duty, and was unable to reach the rest of the family because of his duties at the harbormaster's office.

We lived in a beautiful and spacious country villa owned by my Aunt Concettina. Her husband was a general in the military, and a doctor, and had succumbed to a mild form of madness that quite literally fascinated me. The villa was owned by the Piazza and Inglese families and had a tower that I had made my favorite reading place. The general would sometimes come to visit me there and ask me to read him the page I was currently engaged in. No sooner would I start to read then he would light a cigarette, lie back on the couch and, with eyes closed, listen attentively. When I was done he would look at me and ask, "Can you explain?" "But what is there to explain", I would reply, "it's Leopardi. He says the night is clear because there's no wind, there's the moon that ..." "Ah, the moon", the general would sigh. Then he would break down and laugh until tears streamed down his face. The word "moon" was one that would send him into extended fits of hilarity. Others were "ant", "heart", and "health". He had been forbidden to smoke, and Aunt Concettina was quite strict about this particular prohibition. Like a truffle-hunting dog she would first sniff out and then dig up cigarettes that her husband had hidden in the most unimaginable places. He was continuously supplied with smokes by a complicit farmhand. One day when my aunt had gone into town, he got himself up in his old World War I general's uniform, blocked a German column on the road outside the villa and demanded that they hand over all cigarettes in their possession. The Germans, impressed no doubt by the uniform, handed over an entire case of them. With the help of the farmhand, he then proceeded to mount the roof of the villa and hide his stash under the tiles. Two days later there was a downpour and my aunt, absolutely stunned, watched a hailstorm of cigarettes descend from the sky.

The soldiers of the Goering Division had decided to camp out in a field on the far side of the road in front of our villa, and it soon became almost impossible to go out of the house, with the Allied forces machine-gunning the field, and the Germans responding with anti-aircraft fire. I used to visit the

Germans often, with a flask of wine that I would barter for some canned goods. Food was scarce by then, and we were used to feeding ourselves with dried fava beans and the eggs of the few hens that hadn't been stolen and boiled by the Germans. Two or three times I was taken by surprise in the field by the small Allied bombs. One day a bomb squarely hit a foxhole that a German soldier had dug for himself, tearing him to pieces. The various body parts were gathered together in a wax covered cloth and buried in the hole made by the explosion, near the dry-wall that flanked the road. His fellow soldiers cried over the primitive wooden cross that bore the soldier's name, surname, rank and serial number. In just a matter of days it was impossible for me to get to the field where the Germans were camped. In addition to the bombing raids, the Germans were under pressure from cannon fire from the Allied forces, who by now must have been quite close by. The whole family had taken refuge in the villa's enormous cellar, and was soon joined by neighboring families, who thought that our cellar was safer than theirs. To make a long story short, we ended up with about twenty people in our cellar. One afternoon, a German lieutenant, who spoke respectable Italian, came to advise us to leave the villa, telling us that the Allied forces were just a few hundred yards away and that hand-to-hand combat, which would involve every one of us, was all but inevitable. After informing us of the situation he promptly left. A brief consultation ensued, at the end of which everyone decided to stay. After all, there were a number of elderly among us, and a sick person who couldn't be moved. We were in possession of around thirty eggs, so my Uncle Massimo, reasoning that the cellar gave on to the kitchen, decided to brave the six or seven steps and boil them. No one knew how long the bombing raids would last. At sundown all hell broke loose: bombs, cannon fire, machine gun fire; obviously the prelude to the hand-to-hand combat the German lieutenant had warned us about. Needless to say we were terrified. The fracas lasted more than two hours, and then suddenly ended. Just as suddenly, we began to hear single fire gunshots, from very near. "They're here", said Uncle Massimo. No one had the nerve to speak and, in the silence that followed, the chattering of teeth could be heard. The gunfire increased and the wait became interminable. The Americans must have some strange rifles, I thought; they had a muted sound, as though they had silencers on them. "I can't take it anymore", my Aunt Concettina cried out in a sudden panic that soon became contagious. All of the women began alternately to cry, pray and scream. Then I saw Uncle Massimo rise and bolt up the stairs, paying no heed to his wife's exhortations. Just seconds after he entered the kitchen the gunfire ceased. And just seconds after that, my uncle reappeared. "That wasn't gunfire", he said. "It was the eggs that were left to boil. They started exploding when the water evaporated". Soon after, we were all deep asleep, exhausted from fear, tension and hunger. I was the only one up at sunset, accompanied by the *ethereal sound of birdsong. They hadn't sung for at least two weeks, and now there was no other sound but their warbling. I went out. There were no Germans to be found, though there were traces of their presence in the burning trucks, sunken tents, and the cross on the grave of the shattered soldier. I had my back to the door of the villa and was meditating on the wisdom of crossing the road and searching the ruins for some canned food. Suddenly I heard a noise on the side of the road that led to Serradifalco, and turned around. An enormous tank, taking up the entire road, was slowly advancing. I had never seen anything like it before. I stood there, paralyzed, watching it move forward. At a certain point the tank moved right to make way for an automobile, the likes of which I had also never seen before. I later learned that it was called a jeep. A black soldier was driving, and next to him was another soldier. Standing behind them in the jeep was a man holding on to a curved bar. When the jeep passed before me, the man in the back tapped on the driver's shoulder to stop. I could see the standing man from up close. He had two belts holding two large revolvers, and a helmet, if I remember correctly, with three small silver flowers on it. He didn't seem to notice me, as his gaze settled on the cross of the German soldier just in front of him. All of a sudden he reached out and ripped it from the ground, broke it over his knee and told the driver to move on. I was horrified by the idiocy and infamy of that gesture, and it scared me much more than the bombings I had lived through the previous days.*

As soon as the tank pulled past me I noticed that behind it were two rows of soldiers, about a dozen in all, their uniforms wrinkled and muddy. They each had a garland of hand grenades around their necks like a Hawaiian lei. They passed by me without a word, their heads down. They were clearly exhausted. One of the last in the row turned back towards me and gave me a military salute. "Hey there, buddy", he said in Sicilian. "He ... hello", I said, terrified. "You got a bit of olive oil, buddy?" "Yeah", I answered. "OK, let me find it here in about a half hour, when we march back. I wanna make some nice Sicilian salad for my captain. I imagine you got lettuce and vinegar, and maybe some salt", he said. He saluted me again and walked off. For some reason I couldn't understand I started crying, feeling something between joy and sadness. When the soldiers returned I had the oil. There were twelve of them, plus the captain, and all of them were sons of Sicilian émigrés. Only the captain was American. While the one who had saluted me was making the salad I told him about what had happened with the cross, and asked him about the man that had done it. "That man's a great general, the best there is", he said. "He's got guts, one of those who marches at the head of any column. But as a man, he's a pile of shit. His name's Patton".

I hadn't had any news about my father, who was still in Porto Empedocle, for more than fifteen days. My mother was nearly out of her mind with worry. After the Allied landing, she had seen a number of

Italian sailors who were retreating and had asked them for news. All of them said the same thing: that Porto Empedocle had been destroyed by heavy bombing and the death toll was high. I couldn't take it anymore. I borrowed the bicycle my Aunt Concettina kept in her house and left for Porto Empedocle with my cousin Alfredo, who was a few years younger than me and also had no news of his family. Alfredo had his own bicycle and had ridden it over to visit us before the Allied landing. It was a beautiful bike from a big manufacturer, and expensive, too. Needless to say, Alfredo was proud of it. My bike, on the other hand, was a Montante.

Porto Empedocle was fifty kilometers away, and after the first one hundred meters we realized that it was going to be an arduous journey. The road was nothing but holes and craters. What's more, it was covered with the twisted parts of auto bodies, large screws, tires that had been run over by heavy tanks, broken glass, rifle pieces, and the remains of Italian and German trucks that had been hit while retreating, the burnt carcasses of which were lying by the side of the road. Alfredo suffered the first flat tire of the trip after around two kilometers, and it dampened our spirits. "If the whole road is like this, we'll never make it", one of us said. We fixed the flat and headed off. The worst was yet to come, and it hit us soon after. All of a sudden we found ourselves in front of a column of tanks and jeeps coming the other way, leaving not even a pinhole for us to pass through. I was riding in front and thought that they would let me pass, which of course they didn't, and off I went on the side of the road. I lost my balance and tumbled a few meters with my bike. Alfredo suffered the same fate, and had another flat tire, to boot.

We lost some more time. The oncoming columns seemed to open up a bit, and we remounted our bikes. Every once in a while, though, they would tighten, and off the road we would fly. About a quarter of the way, Alfredo had his third flat tire. At that point I decided to leave him behind, given that my bike was riding like a dream: no flats, no twisted spokes, no bent handlebars, the chain in perfect shape. I headed off on my own. Every so often I would talk to my bike, "Yeah, that's it. Good girl. Just keep riding, just keep riding", I said, caressing the crossbar as though it were the mane of a horse. I stopped occasionally: at times because I was tired, at others to get a better look at something that struck me. At one point I passed through a landscape that looked straight out of Dante's Inferno. Dozens and dozens of uprooted trees, burnt dry by fire, leaving dark holes on the blackened ground, and not a reed of grass or any living thing left. It was the scene of a tank fight, and five or six of our tanks were left there, gutted. Hanging from the turret of one was the corpse of a soldier who hadn't made it out in time. His jacket had fallen and covered his face. A packet of letters had fallen from his jacket pocket. I picked them up and promised myself to make sure they got, one way or another, to his loved ones. There were more bodies near the other tanks, and an unbearable stench in the late July sun that baked men, animals and plants. I took off again, and as I was riding I stripped off my pants, shirt and undershirt and threw them to the wind. I was riding along in nothing but my underpants and sandals. Sure, it was hot, but there was another reason, one that eluded me at the time, and though it was there inside of me, I couldn't get a handle on it. I felt it was that obscure reason, more than the anxiety I had about my father, that kept me pedaling despite the physical and psychological fatigue, despite the thirst. My canteen was empty by then, and had gone the same way as my clothes. I stopped only once, to ask a farmer for a drink of water, and after that I didn't want to waste any more time. I was just outside the city of Agrigento when I saw something written on the wall surrounding a hut. It was written in green paint with large block letters. It said LONG LIVE FREEDOM. It was then that I understood why I had been freeing myself of my clothes as I rode. A slogan like that might seem rhetorical today, but it was wasn't back then. I had felt the need to greet this new and long awaited reality unclothed, as one would a second birth. If possible, I would have stripped myself of my old skin. Once I got to Agrigento I ran into a relative of mine, and called his name. I don't think we had ever really liked each other that much, but we immediately hugged and carried on like two brothers who had survived a shipwreck.

"Have you heard anything about my father", I asked him, as my heart skipped a beat. "Yes, I went to Porto Empedocle yesterday and I saw him", he replied. I felt my legs turning into ricotta cheese, and could barely keep standing. My whole body was spent. I remounted my bike, but after just a few meters, and for no plausible reason, I fell to the ground. For the first time, after all the spills I had taken on the trip, I hurt myself. I walked my bike to the seashore, except there was no sea. It had been replaced by a mass of iron and steel: by hundreds of ships, side by side for as far as the eye could see. They were all waiting to unload materiel for the Allied forces. I was stunned. There was a man standing next to me in silence. "You could walk from here to Tunisia", he said suddenly. Luckily, the road that led from Agrigento to my town was almost all downhill but, because it couldn't be taken by bicycle, I walked. I passed hundreds of amphibians carrying armaments from the ships to the warehouses, transforming themselves from boats into tanks. They dumped water from their keels, covering the paving stones with half a meter of mud. There was an enormous sign on a house that said, in broken Italian: WHOEVER FINDS BOMBES, OR OTHER UNEXPLODED DEVISES, NOT TO TOUCH THEM, BUT TO BRING THEM TO THE COMAND OFFICE. The people in my town were a little confused. "If we can't touch them, how are we supposed to bring them to the command office?" they wondered. I found my father in the harbormaster's office. The Americans had put him in charge of civilian affairs at the port and had made him a harbormaster. He was busy when I found him and couldn't leave work. I de-

cided to walk home. I badly needed to bathe, and to lie down on a bed. But when I arrived there was a long line of American soldiers outside the door, each of them armed with a cake of soap and a towel. They had discovered that my house was one of the few that had a bathtub and shower, and they were using them to the fullest. Because almost all of them were second-generation Sicilian-Americans, I explained who I was, and they immediately put me at the head of the line. When I walked in I saw that there was not a single piece of furniture: not a mirror, not an armchair, not even a book. Nothing. Later, my father told me that vandals had taken advantage of the bombardments and the ensuing chaos and had made off with everything. He had managed to find an army cot for himself, and one for me. It was on that cot that I had one of the deepest sleeps of my life. When I woke up the next day, for some inexplicable reason, the temples of Agrigento came to mind. I was sure that the bombings had damaged them, and wanted to see them and check for myself. I got on my bike and started pedaling. I don't know how I managed to make it through the uphill ride of The Catena, because all the previous day's fatigue suddenly hit me again. From that altitude, the port was a Babylonia of ships and amphibians, with ships waiting to land for as far as the eye could see. What's more, there were dozens and dozens of enormous balloons suspended in the air to prevent a close-range air attack.

At this point I was swerving on my bike. A black American soldier took pity and loaded me and my bike in his jeep. He left me at the bottom of the Temple of the Concordia. In the blinding morning light the temple seemed to be intact. Just in front of the temple there was an American soldier taking photos. Or at least he was trying to. He would frame the shot, then shake his head and move to his left, frame again and shake his head and move to the right. At one point he started running, then stopped and looked for another angle. Even then he didn't seem satisfied. I looked at him in wonder. There was the temple, all you had to do was photograph it, I thought. What was he looking for? I took him for a Sicilian; he had all the physical traits. Maybe he was looking for a little souvenir to take back to his relatives in America.

At that exact moment, we were deafened by the sound of airplanes and shots. Looking up we saw a duel between a low-flying German plane and an equally low-flying American one. I threw myself on the ground. The American soldier also threw himself on the ground, except that he was belly-up. He was shooting photos one after the other, with no hint of indecision. The camera, in his hands, was a weapon, a machine gun. Suddenly both planes disappeared. We both got up, and I said something to him in Sicilian dialect. He didn't understand. I didn't speak English, but I understood a few words. He told me he was a war photographer. He wrote his name on a piece of paper: Robert Capa. I had no idea who he was at the time. I got back on my bike and the whole road was downhill. Now, when I happen to see one of Capa's Sicilian photos, I can smell the fragrances of those days, hear the sounds, the words, the noises.

I stayed in town for twenty-four hours and then, dressed to resemble an American deserter, I headed back to Serradifalco. It took me much more time to get back than it took me to arrive. The tension had disappeared, but the heat and the fatigue had not. The roads were in worse shape. Thousands of Allied vehicles had ripped open new holes and left more metallic debris. Yet, my wonderful bicycle didn't get a single flat tire. Faithful and tough, the only signs of wear that it bore from that difficult trip were some scrapes on the black paint. I proudly gave it back to Aunt Concettina and was sure that I would never see it again. Years later I learned that that bike was made in a craftsmen's factory in Serradifalco. So I feel it only right to offer my sincere and grateful thanks to that precious and irreplaceable friend in those tragic times: the Montante bicycle.

ANDREA CAMILLERI

Calò's Big Sprint

As always, there was a legend. This was an old story, three centuries old. They say that every seven years, at midnight on the dot, there is a magical fair in the small piazza near the Testa dell'Acqua Fountain. Whoever wanted to participate had to get up on the edge of the fountain and wait. Before the church bells ring twenty-four times, the whole piazza will become as bright as day, as if by magic. The piazza fills with cows, goats and sheep. Sellers hawk their goods: work tools, wooden sieves, bread bins, pitchforks, hoes, rope and saddles. Others sell apples, oranges, pomegranates, carobs, grapes, quinces, eggplant and tomatoes. A crowd gathers and crosses paths, but no one sells and no one buys. It's a silent and airy marketplace. It's the fair that celebrates the Day of the Dead, everyone says, but few have seen it. Whoever is able to buy even a single piece of fruit becomes the king or queen of the fair, and acquires great wealth, because the fruit turns into gold. But this happens every seven years. You have be very lucky and very quick on your feet to take part in the fair, and to buy your fortune.

There is a boy who knows the legend. He's heard it told many times. It's one of the town's stories, a town that lies between the mountains, the plain, Lake Soprano and the sierras where hawks fly, in a panorama broken up by white rock, sulfur springs and arid countryside, with sultry summers and humid winters. Serradifalco is a faraway place, far away from everything: the sea, the big cities, the main lines of communication. It's a town of few roads, with few churches, houses made of plaster, and a short history. Founded in 1653 by the Palermitano Baron Leonardo Lo Faso, Serradifalco counted 457 inhabitants in 75 houses in its first census. A village lost in the feudal desolation of central Sicily, roughly twenty kilometers from Caltanissetta, Serradifalco, in name and custom, reveals its Arabic origins – Qalat-an-Nissa: the castle of women, the town of concubines and honey and sesame-seed sweets, nougat, almonds and pistachios served by the concubines for the Berber warriors. Together with Enna, Serradifalco was the last line of Arab resistance to the Norman conquest.

The Boy and the Moon

It's hard to know what a boy born in Serradifalco in 1908 can imagine. We can presume that he knows quite a bit about his family, particularly in a place where the past tends to reconnect to the present, at times to both condition and spoil him.

Calogero Montante was named after his paternal grandfather, though in Sicily the giving of names is capricious and complex. Calogero is a saint who is particularly revered in the provinces of Agrigento and Caltanissetta. It is possible that St. Calogero was originally African, and he is depicted in churches with either a white or black face. He has always been fanatically venerated in central and southern Sicily; so venerated, in fact, that local folklore maintains that 450 years after the birth of Christ, seven Calogeros, brothers all, some with light skin, some with dark, roamed southern Sicily. From the name Calogero we have the derivative names Caliddu, Calò, Calorio, Lillo, Lilliddu, Luzzo, Lillì, Gero, Lillinè, Rino, Rirì, and so on, and so on, to the point at which we lose any etymological significance on one's birth certificate.

What did Calò Montante imagine at the age of seven, or ten, or eleven? Who knows what he thought while looking at the sky and the moon above the sulfur mines of Serradifalco, the same sky and moon that Pirandello had Ciàula discover while making his way out of the mine shaft. He certainly knew that he was growing up in a land of ancient poverty, among mountains of misery, in the midst of dark and closed suffering, in the bowels of the earth. Where Serradifalco descends towards the valley, the trails leading to the sulfur mines open up. The mines of Serradifalco and San Cataldo had terrifying names, like Rabbione,

Giulfo, Stincone, Apaforte, Marici, and Dragaito. From the sierras of the falcon, the large rock formations that give definition and identity to the town, one could see the vastness of the high sulfur plains that extend from Caltanissetta to Aragona in a hellish nativity scene gravid with fumes, unbreathable air, teeming humanity, and an undertone of violence. This was a land of bullying wagon drivers, drunken pickaxers, workers with bent and sore backs, an ascendant Mafia, and economic blackmail. From the sierras of the falcon, one's eye would take in a Dantesque ring of towns: Sutera, Racalmuto, Canicattì, San Cataldo, Montedoro, Bompensiere, and Milena, with their arid hills, littered with the detritus of the mines and scarred with their dark entranceways, wagon rails and the furnaces that burned through the night.

This is a landscape that has something of the absolute about it, etched in stone and sky like certain engravings by Domenico Faro. A landscape of despairing beauty, as the eye takes in the yellow hills covered with grain, stone walls and green patches of almond groves, under an implacable light. This is a panorama capable of expressing the words written by Sebastiano Aglianò in his *Che cos'è questa Sicilia (What is This Sicily)*, from 1945: "In Sicily you feel like you have finally touched the earth. All of the subtleties find expression here, degrees of fogginess, atmospheric uncertainties, and all of a sudden absolute and essential tones emerge... prickly pears clinging to cliffs, and virulent agave plants under a noon sun wear the mind down to the point of hallucination. The brightest colors blind the eye and impede contemplative meditation, though they bring sight to a sweet state of repose. Close them for a minute and your eyes will see nothing, absolutely nothing, even if you reach deep into your mind. Open them and you realize the universe is there above you, implacable". And then, "There is a clarity in nature that rocks the soul". Aglianò's conclusion is trenchant: "If you're looking for absolute objectivity, this is the world for you".

This scenario is similar to the one in which Tomasi di Lampedusa's Chevally di Monterzuolo, from Piedmont, moved when he landed in Sicily. "He looked: all around him, under the ashen light, the landscape lurched and jostled, irredeemable". In *Il Gattopardo* (*The Leopard*), even the landscape becomes "the worst tyrant of mankind". It is, as the Prince of Salina explains, "[A] landscape that ignores points between the lascivious and the parched, that is never moderate, measured or distended, as a landscape for rational beings should be".

From the valleys of Serradifalco, from this absolute and irredeemable landscape, the sulfur miners would emerge, a lost look in their eyes, half naked from work, with death on their mind and a tremor in their hands. They brought news from the underground: stories sparked with sudden flames, explosions wrought from a pickaxe on stone, gas trapped in the mountain faults. They would be washed to safety by flood waters in the galleries, waters that would drown men, money and business deals. They would walk up to town, finding the road lined with worried women at the beginning of the trail to the mines. Images that get confused with those in black and white from Luchino Visconti's *La terra trema* (*The Earth Trembles*) with its black scarves waving in the wind from the reefs of Acitrezza. But film is art, and life is only joy or sorrow.

On the crags of clay and marl, the women of Serradifalco, the wives and daughters and mothers of miners, anxiously await the survivors of the latest tragedy. After the hugs and embraces, when almost all of them have returned, their hair wet with death and salvation, some women – one only, or two or three or five – will remain on the side of the trail, their eyes fixed on the already deserted mine and the dead buried within. At this point in the cruel game of victims and survivors, it will be time to dry the tears, because there will be no more miners making their way up with the hill. Who knows how many times Calò Montante heard the dark screams of the wives and daughters and mothers of miners. You grow up in Sicily and you grow up with the idea of death, feel affection for it. It is the dead, in November, who bring sweets, sugar babies, dried fruit and some wooden toys for the children. It is the dead who pass through town at the ringing of the church bells. A child doesn't think about death. A boy thinks about climbing the Testa dell'Aqua Fountain at the stroke of midnight to buy the golden fruit that will make him rich. Every child has a dream. Calò has one, and who knows how it got there. He wants to go fast, on the streets and country roads of Serradifalco, with the wind in his hair and a squint in his eyes. Fast as blood pumping into muscle. Calò wants to go faster than anyone.

Photos of Milady

Let's turn on the time machine and enter Serradifalco in 1908. And let's do it together with an elegant woman from a foreign land. Born in Nice, France, the daughter of an Irishman who left the United Kingdom because of a feud with the Scottish and English branches of his family, Louise Hamilton grew up in Florence. It was there that she met Eugenio Caico, the scion of the richest and most influential family in Montedoro, a town just ten kilometers from Serradifalco. Because of a complicated history of family jealousy, Louise and Eugenio were never able to set foot in Sicily, much less in the town where the Caico ruled. But, in 1897, after almost a decade, the ostracism ceased. Thus is was that Louise Hamilton Caico discovered central Sicily, the part of the island that travelers avoid and foreigners ignore.

Louise Hamilton often traveled around Monte-doro by carriage, accompanied by the Caico family's horsemen, dressed in fustian, with the Sicilian cap known as the *coppola*, and a shotgun slung over the shoulder. Milady, on the other hand, was armed with a simple camera, a rarity at that time. In 1910 her excursions and her Sicilian experience eventually became a book entitled *Sicilian Ways and Days*, stock full of anecdotes, and recounted with a distinctly British sense of irony. Let's enter Serrad-ifalco with milady and observe her photos.

"As soon as we entered the town I was immediately taken by the entrance to the inn that was to host us", she writes. "From an iron bar above the door there hung the most assorted items and wares. First in line was an amber coloured ampho-ra, to signal that the inn served as a tavern. Next in line were some potatoes and a handful of *mac-cheroni* to indicate the sale of food. A shirt and collar were blowing in the breeze, proclaiming that here one could also find articles of cloth-ing. A leather belt was hanging at the end of the line. After carefully observing the sign above the inn, we entered".

The inn was humble, indeed: a short step above a hostel. It was both a store and a tavern. "In the corner was a large amphora with a slot into which the most generous imbibers could insert offer-ings to St. Joseph, a very popular figure in this area. His effigy, dressed in the brightest of colours, hangs from the round part of the amphora. Near the bar was an engraved wooden trunk, the dowry of a good part of the Sicilian brides of the less fortunate classes, containing the wardrobe of the entire family. A child was rocking in a small rocking chair. At the far end was a door that led into a large kitchen, where men were seated at food and drink, and where the host and his family slept in a large bed".

The innkeeper ("a most attractive young man, well shaven, carefully dressed, with the aspect of an elegant coachman and the manners of a gentleman") together with his wife, welcomed milady, ("large almond-shaped eyes and a sweet smile"). Suspecting that they were in the presence of illustrious company, the innkeeper offered the foreigner and her armed escort the upper floor. Louise had traveled to Serradifalco for lunch, having heard that one ate well in the town. In fact, "Lunch, served in a variety of courses, was good and unusual. We began with salami, then moved on to stuffed artichokes, vegetables, rock-hard pork chops and, finally, green beans, salad and cheese. The courses were served without rhyme or reason, in no particular order, though the wine from Syracuse that flowed was absolutely perfect".

After lunch, the group took a postprandial stroll. On her walk, Louise Hamilton stopped at a small shop that sold local terracotta. As she was making her purchase, "a small group of people gathered to observe the lady buying 'low brow things'". Inside, the shop owner, taking advantage of the British woman's eccentric tastes, was certainly not offering low brow prices. On her way back to the carriage, Louise stopped at the Testa dell'Acqua Fountain, the fountain of legend. "The women had formed a queue to fill their water pitchers. The appearance of a woman with a camera provoked surprise and wonder. An understandable reaction when one stops to think that the greatest degree of independence to which a woman here can aspire consists in going to church, wrapped in a shawl from head to foot; and never alone, mind you, but always under the vigilant eye of her handmaid".

Louise Hamilton's photographs reveal an archaic world, frozen in time, an enchanted world. Louise remembers her return to Montedoro "in the deepest silence of the hills and the vast plains, hot and golden under the dying rays. And in the peaceful solitude of the plains of grain, the blue sky seemed to be of a deeper blue, the light, and the heart, lighter".

The Good Fortune of Being Born Rich

Calò didn't know hunger, or what it was like to work in the mines. In contrast to other eight-year-olds in his town who were already looking for tools left behind at harvest time, or carrying loads of sulfur on their backs, Calò was fortunate enough to be born into a family that was well off.

His father, Luigi Montante, was born in 1874 and was an enterprising man who inherited a comfortable legacy that he increased through real estate, commerce in grains, and investments in mining. To get some sense of the Montante family's wealth one need only read the wedding contract signed by Luigi Montante and his future wife, Gaetana Butera, on May 31, 1903 in the office of notary public Rosario Crucillà in Serradifalco. In looping calligraphy the notary certified that "the above-mentioned Gaetana Butera and Luigi Montante have declared before me that, attracted by mutual affection for each other, they are intent on entering into matrimony. It has also been established before me that the same persons intend to establish, as in effect is established with the present act, the civil conditions and regulations that should constitute their conjugal union".

The compromise between the parties was one that existed for all marriages. For the poorest it took the form of a private contract, called a *pitazzo*, which listed household goods such as towels, sheets, bed covers, blankets and table ware, all to be brought to the union by the bride. For the richer classes it involved entire chapters in which the affection and sentiments that were to unite the spouses were described. It also revealed the nest of interests and alliances that the two families were to consolidate through matrimony. For the marriage of Luigi and Donna Gaetana, the father of the bride stipulated that he would invest the bride with "the sum of two hundred lire, as the price of linens and fine furniture, goods to be sold to the future husband, Luigi Montante, who, upon declaring receipt thereof, will provide to the endower the analogous sum, in accordance with the law".

In addition, the bride's mother promised another two hundred lire, in cash, to be given within two years of the wedding, on the condition that it be invested by Luigi in a piece of real estate. Regulations and fine print, provisions for non-compliance, and correctives were all covered in the greatest detail. It should be noted that in this part of Sicily there is great passion for legalese, court rulings and juridical subtlety. Trying to foresee every possibility was merely a way of avoiding litigation, the basis of which is to be found in the complexity of the prenuptial contracts. Litigation would end up in court, with cases that would drag on for decades. In the meantime, resentment and family rivalries would boil, hatreds would endure, positions would shift, and affection and inheritance would go up in smoke. Unless, of course, things could be resolved quickly and conveniently in a land where, as Leonardo Sciascia once said, one can pass quickly from a land survey to ballistic forensics: the sound of a shotgun from behind a stone wall, the rival taken care of, and off you go.

This was not the case with the Montante family, who well understood the complexities of familial relations, especially when the family is also a business enterprise. In any case, and against all misfortune, the sixth article of the nuptial contact between Luigi and Gaetana states that the dowry would remain with Luigi "both in the case that his future wife precede him in death, and that his future wife and her descendants precede him in death". Fortunately, that eventuality would remain on paper only. Luigi and Gaetana would spend fifty-three years of married life together, survive two world wars, and weather the small battles that accompany every long marriage.

If You Have to Choose between Life and Death, Choose America

Calò was born into a family that had a relatively easy life. It is chance that aids some and ails others, particularly when destiny can depend on birthright. No biography can recount the thoughts of a child of a century ago. But we can try to imagine the small joys and fears that always accompany childhood: night and darkness. Here we can turn to a writer from this part of Sicily, a man of Calò's age, born in Montedoro, a stone's throw from Serradifalco. His name is Angelo Petyx. His 1957 novel *La miniera occupata* (*The Occupied Mine*) is a chronicle of the cultural and political awakening of a young miner. Here, Petyx describes the melancholy that comes with insomnia: "I looked beyond the rooftops and out over the peak of Mount Ottavio and thought that when I was a child I believed that that was all I needed to do to fill my pocket with stars. But I was afraid to go out at night and gather my stars, and so there I would sit on my small balcony, putting off my adventures until the night came in which the big bad wolf would no longer scare me. So here I am now, no longer afraid of the wolf, except that the stars, my lovely childhood stars, were no longer roosting on the peak of Mount Ottavio, but were far, far away. Who knows where or why".

Big bad wolves inhabit every corner of the big world, of which even Serradifalco is a part. History with a capital H would come to wreak havoc on the Montante family. At the age of forty, with a wife, two children, and a number of business activities, Luigi was called to arms. After all, war is war, and there were no reasons to look for shortcuts in order not to serve. Italy became a depopulated country, with young men at the front, bad news from the north of the country, and telegrams full of mourning for the fallen soldiers in the trenches of the world war. When Luigi returned from the front in 1918 he found a town that was even more bled by misery, impoverished and fragile. Serradifalco's population of ten thousand was reduced by death and emigration. The mines were experiencing the first wave of an irreversible crisis that fifty years later would bring them to a halt. Many of the town's residents were to take the steamship from Palermo heading west, towards America.

The rooms and halls of Ellis Island are now empty. The only sounds to be heard are those of tourists following the itinerary that was obligatory for the immigrants who arrived from Europe. But that wasn't what it was like a century ago. In the ongoing confusion of every docking, in the midst of the modest possessions that now fill the showcases, the lost gazes of those who had chosen to leave everything behind in order to start over again fell on American immigration officials. Clutching letters of invitation from family or friends, men and women who spoke more dialect than Italian tried desperately to pronounce the name of their town or village of origin, names that for every one of them were nothing more than a handful of houses, of affections, faces, pain, poverty and nostalgia.

Between 1901 and 1920, the surname Montante was repeated seventy-one times in the now sunny rooms of Ellis Island. From the large windows that looked out over the Hudson River, one could barely see the skyscrapers of downtown Manhattan. This was the mirage that the Italian film maker Emanuele Crialese captured in the final scene of his 2006 film *Nuovomondo (The Golden Door)*. Men of forty, young men of twenty, and sixty-year-old women, gave their names and surnames to be registered in the archives of Ellis Island. Those archives are the palimpsest of an entire nation that arrived by sea. And how many children there were! Babies wrapped in blankets, or just learning how to walk: babies who would remember nothing of Sicily. In front of immigration officers and their interpreters (among whom was Fiorello La Guardia, who would become New York's first Italian-American mayor) the surname Montante was given seventy-one times. The name of the town of origin was sometimes mangled in transcription, according to how it was pronounced. So, we have these variations on a theme: Serradifolco, Lerradifalco, Lenadifolco, Serradifalo, Serrafalco, Serradifales. Thus transcribed, the town seems even more distant. Lost forever.

Luigi was one of the Montantes who had no need to emigrate, unlike others who bore the same name and who were, in some cases, cousins or distant relatives. Luigi was able to make a new start for himself and his family with his land holdings. He started up the Montante Brothers Company in order to manage the family assets without affecting the existing plans for inheritance. These were not easy years and, perhaps inevitably, there were disagreements, equivocations, misunderstandings. One gets a sense of these difficulties in a letter dated September 7, 1933 and sent by Luigi to his brother Peppino, who was working and living in Rome at the time. "Remember that our name is Montante, and people have always held us in high regard. Now, everyone is talking about us. Dear brother, let's see eye to eye, let's help each other out, let's love each other. We are blood, and the good Lord will compensate us".

The letter did little good, and in 1937 the family company was dissolved, with each of the brothers taking his piece of the estate and moving on separately.

Dawn in Piazza Loreto

It's much too easy to look at life in the glow of retrospect; to see in a confluence of stars, dates and coincidences the key to an interpretation of a life. Yet it was two wheels, two pedals and a chain that gave Calò the necessary push to overcome his immediate surroundings, his world. A world that would, in the end, belong to him. So how can one ignore the casual meshing of events, if those events end up conditioning life and its choices? Calò was not even born when the Milan-based sports paper *La Gazzetta dello Sport*, published three times a week, announced on August 7, 1908 that the first Giro d'Italia would take place the following year.

In fact, at 2:53 a.m. on May 13, 1909, one hundred and twenty-seven cyclists, atop heavy bikes, with inner tubes on their shoulders, pedaled out of the fog of Milan's Piazza Loreto to inaugurate the very first Giro d'Italia, a course that covered 2,448 kilometers. Of those at the starting line, only forty-nine would cross the finish line back in Milan. The winner, Luigi Ganna, after having ridden 89 hours and 48 minutes, won the race, worth 5,325 lire. The last-place finisher took home 300 lire, not a bad consolation prize in those days. The first Giro can be summed up in these few numbers. It was the beginning of an adventure that would last the rest of the century, and continues to this day, with its scandals, disappointments and chemical trickery.

Calò was just a few months old when the Giro debuted, knowing nothing of life or of bicycles. He didn't know, for example, that 1,000 of the 25,000 lire in prize money was offered by Vincenzo Florio, the scion of the Palermitan Florio family. Vincenzo was in the habit of spending money and lending the prestige of his family name to racing events of all sorts. He was also the younger brother of Ignazio Florio, whose life and decline defined the most luxurious and most tragic epoch of the Sicilian entrepreneurial dream. Vincenzo was the typical English sportsman. He loved gambling and speed, and relished a good challenge. He had good intuition and the money to back it up. He seemed to intuit that car racing, bicycle racing and aviation (indeed, all of the mechanical and technological advances that marked the beginning of the 20th century) had the potential to become competitive sports. He also understood that tying the name of an important industrial empire to sporting events gave returns on investment in terms of visibility and prestige. This was before the idea of sponsorship had developed, though the concept was essentially the same. Of course, Vincenzo did all this in inimitable Sicilian style, with an aristocratic disdain for balance sheets (which never balanced), a cavalier attitude towards revenues and outlays, and a bold disinterest towards those who advised him to surround himself with what today would be called a managerial team. This was the pioneering age of the first Targhe Florio – the first auto-racing events, and the first bicycle races, which Vincenzo had organized in 1907, two years before the first Giro. Needless to say, these were pastimes for the rich.

According to the annuals of the Touring Club Italiano, there were just fifty-two automobiles registered in Sicily in 1904, less than half those found on the streets of Rome at the time, and just a quarter of those registered in Milan. And if some cars were seen on the streets of Palermo, where at least thirty-six were registered (some of them belonging to Vincenzo Florio), in the entire province of Caltanissetta there was just one, which belonged, for the record, to Giuseppe Giordano. To find another, one had to look eighty kilometers south, to Agrigento, where a car was made available to the clients of the high-class Hotel des Temples.

In a scenario like this, organizing auto races was truly a risky undertaking. It was done on a wave of enthusiasm, and by recruiting friends from the world of Sicilian aristocracy, populated in part by penniless men who lived a life of luxury, often at the expense of the Florio family. There were races, and high times, good food and a flood of French champagne. After all, when it was all over, the bill was sent to the Florio headquarters, where Ignazio bit his tongue and paid. *Noblesse oblige*.

The years passed by quickly, as did the Giro d'Italia. These were Giros that ran only in continental Italy. In 1911, the cyclists made it as far south as Naples. Southern Italy was a sort of no-man's land. The Italy south of Rome was *in partibus infidelium* (the land of the unbelievers), an arid land, where if there weren't lions (as the ancient maps had it) there were other ferocious beasts. In fact, on the stage between Caserta and Naples the caravan of cyclists came face to face with a herd of buffalos and had to detour onto the grazing fields to get away. After Portici, the race had to be suspended because there were no roads, just foot paths and mule trails.

The Giro was suspended for the First World War. For four years, bicycles were ridden by soldiers and sharpshooters back and forth to the front. But in 1919, with a race that started on May 21 and ended on June 8, the Giro was back in business, organized by the *Gazzetta dello Sport*. It was in this race that a diminutive Ligurian from Novi Ligure made his racing debut. He was 26 years old, had a friend who would become a famous bandit, and a name that would end up defining an entire era of bike racing: Costante Girardengo. In order to live, the Giro needs its legends, its myths, its heroes of endurance. In short, it needs its symbols.

The Birth of a Champion, and of a Bandit

In the Fascist Italy of censured newspapers and expurgated crime reporting in the name of assuring Italians that they could sleep "with unlocked doors", few knew that in addition to the sports hero Costante Girardengo, Novi Ligure was also the hometown of an antihero. Sante Pollastro was six years younger than the cyclist, and the two knew each other, as was to be expected in a small town like Novi Ligure at the turn of the century, where everyone knew everyone else, as well as everyone else's business. They had friends in common, and a common love: bicycles. For Costante, bicycles were a way of moving up in the world. For Sante, they helped him to pull off his robberies. Sante Pollastro had a juvenile record at the age of thirteen. At seventeen, he was a full-fledged criminal, riding and shooting, targeting his prey despite a lazy eye. Sante was a bandit and a bit of a rebel, anarchic and romantic, and between 1922 and 1927, he took particular pleasure in killing policemen and others in uniform, the incarnation of a State that he considered the enemy. He was, however, a fan of Costante's, and it was this, perhaps, that sealed his fate. He was arrested in Paris, where he had traveled to meet his idol, who was riding in the Tour de France. He had confessed to Costante that he was responsible for a murder for which two innocent men had been imprisoned. Girardengo later testified at Sante's trial, for which he would subsequently be suspected of having betrayed the bandit. Sante served thirty-two years, and was released in 1959 at the age of eighty. He went back to Novi Ligure to live out the years left to him. As Marco Ventura, the author of *Il campione e il bandito* (*The Champion and the Bandit*), notes: "He was a scapegoat, the emblem of a price paid in the name of progress and transformation. It was the end of his glory and his luck".

This was Girardengo's other story. The story of a reversal of fortune; the other side of the coin. A bike for both, riding to win, riding to escape. These were parallel lives that would later be evoked in a 1993 song by Francesco De Gregori's brother, Luigi Grechi, and sung by De Gregori. Calogero Montante's grandson Antonello played it for the old man, who was still lucid and curious about things. Who knows if Grandpa Calò was moved (though he probably wouldn't have confessed to it) by hearing those two names reemerge from the past. "Two kids from the neighborhood who grew up too fast / their love of bicycles meant to last / The crossing of fates in a strange history, that now escapes our collective memory / A story from other times, before the driving glove, when races were rage or races were love / But between rage and love gaps grow, and who the winner will be, we already know / Ride Girardengo, ride, there's no one behind you catching up / Ride Girardengo, ride, Sante is out of sight / Behind the curve he hides, fading in the night".

The Blacksmith of Serradifalco

And what happened to Calò? Well, for one thing he started to grow. He grew into a slim and muscular youth, not very tall, but well built. Though he applied himself well at school, he really wanted to work. He loved to read and keep up on things. He devoured technical manuals, newspapers and journals. He liked knowing about things, how they worked, what made their mechanisms click. This isn't to say that he was a mama's boy or a teacher's pet. Latin and Italian grammar bored him, but when there was something practical, something that had an everyday application, his attention was sharp.

You can't expect a boy from Serradifalco, however curious and attentive, to read *Le Figaro*. However, given that ideas often proceed by osmosis, which means that one can be a Freudian without ever having read Freud, one can imagine that Calò felt something in the air of his time, even in Serradifalco, something that had to do with Futurism, which had already influenced Italian art and literature. It was, in fact, in the pages of the Parisian daily in 1909, the year of the first Giro d'Italia if we're looking for affinities and recurrences, that Filippo Tommaso Marinetti published his *Manuale futurista*. Here are some of Marinetti's disingenuous and cutting words: "We affirm that the magnificence of the world is enriched by a new beauty, the beauty of speed. We want to sing of the man at the wheel, the ideal axis of which crosses the earth, and is itself hurled along its orbit". A few years later, and perhaps a bit too convinced of his ideas, Marinetti, together with Mario Sironi, Umberto Boccioni, Luigi Russolo and Antonio Sant'Elia, went happily to the front on his bicycle, dodging enemy bullets and pedaling. Those who survived the war, "the world's only hygiene", dedicated poetry and paintings to the bicycle.

Not even The Prophet missed the war. With his usual bombast, Gabriele D'Annunzio dedicated some of his verses to the constitution, in 1894, of the first sharpshooter cyclist corps. Some of these verses can still be read on the monument to the sharpshooters in Piazza Porta Pia in Rome: "Every spoke of my wheel is tempered by courage and by the circle, always upright, splendid, Lady Fortune without the blindfold". Maybe Calò, without knowing much about Futurism or D'Annunzio, began to cultivate that passion at the anvil of his uncle's blacksmith shop, where he had decided to continue his studies. Calò had abandoned books in favor of the forge and bellows. These were studies in bronze and steel, the sawing of metal, finishing work on the lathe, and elbow grease. Futuristically speaking, if one can put it that way, Calò entered into his own iron age.

Go Binda, Go!

The pink paper is always the same. All you have to do is approach a newsstand to see it, there among the other daily papers printed black on white. Even the reader at the furthest remove from the tension of sports feels a shudder, a hidden thrill. For more than one hundred years, those pink pages have recounted great and small sporting events, and they surely contain less pain, fewer afflictions and agonies than what is recounted in all the other dailies. If it's true that reading the newspaper is the layman's way of praying, the sheer mass of absurd atrocities and unpunished evil found in the daily paper must surely transform prayer into daily supplication. By now, this form of prayer is the citizen's daily dose of spice, with petty scandals, incomprehensible political maneuvers, and repugnant crimes of ordinary folly. Indignation is replaced with resignation, and emotion prevails over information.

But the *Gazzetta* still offers dreams, despite the scandals involving doping, antidoping, rigged soccer games, and corrupt referees and line judges. It often offers drama and melodrama, without the tragic or bloody ending. At times all it takes is a medal won by an obscure fencer, or a humble marathon runner, or a precocious athlete, or an unlucky cyclist, and the pages fly, and the readers with them. There are never enough adjectives; comparisons are all over the place, and metaphors fight for elbow room. To glorify a victory, or exorcize a defeat, the sportswriters invoke the names of ancient Greek heroes, gladiators from the Roman Coliseum, invincible generals. Here in the pink pages, Achilles and Hector, Hannibal and Scipio Africanus, live again.

La Gazzetta dello Sport was sold in Serradifalco in the first decades of the last century. It recounted the duels between Costante Girardengo and Learco Guerra. This was world-class racing at the beginning of the world, when shifting gears and changing tires was the work of first-generation mechanics. There were stories of rivalries and friendships that played themselves out in the valleys and mountains of an Italy that came to discover itself through the Giro. In Serradifalco, people heard the names of cities they had never seen, cities that marked the starting and finishing lines of the various stages: Lucca, Chieti, Macerata. In the *Gazzetta* and other journals, Calò saw photographs of the riders, covered with sweat and mud as they climbed, their arms raised in victory as they crossed the finish line. Calò Montante dreamed of becoming a champion bike racer, with the pink jersey, like Girardengo or Brunero. Or like Binda.

Oh yes, Binda. Alfredo Binda, born in 1902, but still almost a kid, just six years older than Calò. Binda was a plasterer from Cittiglio, near Varese, and had emigrated to Nice, in France. Though he was not very well educated (the only book he had ever read was Manzoni's *I promessi sposi* [*The Betrothed*]), he was a devout reader of newspapers. The Giro needed Binda, with his careful reserve and apparent coldness, to give Italy the figure that would project the event into the sphere of myth and invincibility. Binda overtook a declining Girardengo, and beat a Guerra who was at the height of his powers. He generated his share of antipathy, and overcame his share of injuries, but in the end he earned his place in the pantheon of cyclists. Calò couldn't help but make him his personal hero. A young man of twenty, living in Serradifalco, who makes his living as a blacksmith and loves to ride bicycles, would be hard pressed not to find something to admire in a quiet and humble cyclist who wins the Giro year after year. Binda came to incarnate the Fascist Italietta of the 1920s, the small Italy of artisans and shopkeepers, the underclass and the working class. The *Italietta* that Fascist ideology wanted to indoctrinate with the exploits of saints, poets and navigators. Luckily, there was Binda.

Calò rode his bike around the crags of Serradifalco, along Lake Soprano, on the rough road to Caltanissetta, in the countryside of Canicattì. He rode in the green of spring and the rust of autumn. He rode under the burning summer sun, and through the wet fog of a part of Sicily that resembles Lombardy, as Elio Vittorini would point out. Calò rode and pretended that he was Binda. He tried to emulate the extraordinary feats of the climber, the silent patience of the long-distance rider, and the final burst of the sprinter. Perhaps the words of the legendary *Corriere della Sera* sportswriter Emilio De Martino rang in his ears: "Watching this climber ride, the fatigue looks easy, navigating the road looks easy, everything looks easy... Here's Binda, sometimes a little unhappy, a little insecure, a little uncertain. He has a delicate temperament, but then he is transformed and his intrinsic class as a rider emerges. At that point the champion in him dominates his moods and character, and he pours ahead". Luckily, there's Binda: the redemption of an Italy that has no saints in heaven, as the Italians say. With no illustrious ancestry, no crowns or swords, no coats of arms. Cycling is the sport of sweat and blood, solitude and silence; eyes down, the thin tires pushed by the metallic strength of muscle. Mile after mile.

"I Remember All My Dreams"

Let's listen to the main character. Let's listen to the voice of Calogero Montante. These are the memories of an older man, when Calò had already become Zì Calò, as everyone called him. He was an old man, and had seen a lot in his lifetime, but how can you forget the summer of your youth?

"World War I was over, and those were tough times", Calogero Montante recounted to an interviewer. "We had to take stock of what had happened and start over. At that time, cycling was a very popular sport. But the roads were in bad shape, with ruts and holes, and flat tires happened all the time. The riders had to do the repairs themselves. There were no derailleurs in those days, so climbing and descending were done in one speed. To change the speed, you had to take the rear wheel off using a system we called 'gear shift' or 'wheel turn.' It was in that period that the first rivalry, between the two strongest riders – Costante Girardengo and Alfredo Binda – was born, two heroes of the time. That was when I realized that bicycles and cycling were a real passion for me".

It was to become a consuming passion. "That was when I started thinking of having a bike that was all my own, though it had been a dream of mine since I was a kid. As I said, those were tough times, and a bicycle was a means of transportation for people with money. A racing bike was considered a real luxury. But my love of bicycles was so great that I built my first one piece by piece. That was the first Montante bicycle, built for my very first race. I remember that the races were organized to run along town streets, and the whole thing was like a festivity, with everyone out to participate. What a thrill that day was. I had the town seamstress make me a woolen jersey with the name Montante stitched by hand. I was ready to go, but I had no idea then that this passion would become my livelihood. I decided to put together a team, the Montante Cycling Team. We trained on the local roads, the whole team. We ate up thousands and thousands of kilometers, pushing ourselves to the limit".

If someone had had a movie camera, we could now look at the grainy, silent, black and white frames, scratched by time. But Calogero Montante's memories are more vivid than any reel of film. "Sometimes we would be out for days at a time, going all the way down to Agrigento. We would take only what was necessary with us: a cape for the rain, a change of shoes and some clean underwear and, most important, the tools we needed for repair work. We kept those tools in a case under the saddle. For food, we took some bread and the fruit we found in the fields, particularly the local prickly pears. Of course we had some sweets with us, like nougat, to help us through the rough patches. The taste of nougat still takes me back to those days. We slept under the stars, hugging our bikes. I can remember that during the training runs, if we met a passerby he would cheer us on as though we were in a race, and the more he cheered us on the faster we went. It was fantastic. I weighed fifty kilos and was in perfect shape. I could really fly on a bike. The experiences I had with my bike were unique for me. I could really enjoy the landscape, and even discovered out-of-the-way places for myself that were incredibly beautiful. It was as if my bike and I were part of that incredible beauty, as if I could enter into the natural world. I was free. That's why for me, bicycles are life".

A Story Like Any Other

This isn't a mystery story. This is the story of a boy who became a man in a Sicily that no longer exists. We could even tell you how it turns out. We could start by telling you, in just a few words, how that boy built his first bicycle and, from there, tell lots of other stories. We could tell you that that boy started a business, a company, a commercial enterprise. And we could give you an oil painting, in natural proportions, hanging in the entranceway of a large industrial group that has its origins with the first bicycle built by Calò in the back of his uncle's blacksmith shop.

And even if we did reveal this (and, in part, we have) what would we be telling you that you don't already know? Apparently, nothing. Because Italy, and indeed the whole world, is full of stories like this. We've heard it all before: the industrious, tenacious artisan who achieves personal wealth for himself and his heirs. How many industrial empires were hatched in some obscure workshop in Turin or Detroit? How many multinational corporations are the offspring of an Atlanta pharmacist who came up with an infusion of coca leaves and cola nuts? At the end of the day, it is the modern capitalist epoch, with its successes and excesses. Without citing the most famous examples, there are tens of thousands of these kinds of stories of industrial success; particularly in Italy, where the company is a family, and the family is a company.

Calò's story, on first reading, seems like so many other stories. It's a story without subplots and surprise endings, especially if the reader knows that the initial stubbornness that went into it resulted in a business that employed hundreds of workers, was technologically innovative, and was able to manage productive reconversions, and other means of production, all of which simply adds up to a company that prospers and profits. Yet there is something singular about this story that almost makes it unique, and that is where it took place: in Serradifalco, in the province of Caltanissetta, Sicily.

Stories like this don't attract attention in the United States, Germany or Great Britain. They don't even attract much attention in places like Brescia, Bergamo, Vicenza or Milan. But Sicily is not the land of Buddenbrooks or Krupps. The

Sicily of Serradifalco, with it sulfur steam and fields of grain, and its archaic system of landownership, knows little of industry and industrialists. Even the sulfur mines, which could have led to some sort of economic system, were run the old fashioned way, with a wild exploitation of resources and labor, old machinery, rapacious commercial practices, and an absolute lack of cooperation between owners and managers. It was never an industry and never would be. It was only a living hell where at the end of the week profits and losses were added up. It was nothing more than poor man's bread.

This is why Calò's story is unique in this latitude. His sprint, to use a cycling term, started slowly, while the fortunes of the Florio family died quickly. An unfair comparison, you might be inclined to say. The Florios are often mentioned as emblems of a possible model of entrepreneurship that Sicily has never really had, or at least only sporadically had. But the Florio experience, in Palermo and in Sicily, was nothing but the dream of industrial omnipotence that groups shipping fleets, factories, mines, the tuna trade, high class hotels and luxury pastimes. The Florios lived in a parallel universe. While Palermo and Sicily were at the center of this industrial dream, the family could count on little else. The Florios were kings of the desert, and that desert was a Sicily with no economic fabric, with no small businesses, no artisanal enterprises. The Florios were not long for this industrial world, and they came to an end because there weren't enough Calò Montantes on the island. If there had been more young men and women who knew how to build bicycles, tend vines, and make things, maybe the Florio's sun would not have set on a mirage-like sea of high society, like the fortunes of so many dukes and barons who detested the Florios while basking in the reflected rays of their fading glory. To survive, the Florios would have had to see their mirror image in the Calò Montantes of this world, and to recognize themselves as the offspring of the same hard-working bourgeois class. They would have needed to build alliances, exalt the work ethic and the logic of production. But in their golden isolation, they opted to surround themselves with aristocratic idleness, proud of its particular brand of illiteracy, and hardheaded in its belief that a princess could decline to sign a document because she was a noblewoman.

Obviously, there were rich people; rich like Mastro Don Gesualdo, whom even Verga treated with a barely veiled disdain. They should have formed the backbone of a regional economy, but they didn't. Perhaps they were rich but insecure, as Leonardo Sciascia described them, writing of the sulfur and salt mine managers in Racalmuto in 1955. This is from Sciascia's *Parrocchie di Regalpetra* (*The Parishes of Regalpetra*): "The self-taught man in matters of wealth stands somewhere between poverty and wealth. He talks like a rich man and acts like a pauper. He despises the rich who have never known poverty, and looks down on the poor who have never figured out how to become rich. This condition of isolation breeds violence, egocentric fury. The wealthy man assumes all of the characteristics of an outlaw, viewing the law as impotent in the face of money, and in the face of the same poor people who have been corrupted by their poverty. This wealthy man is an outlaw armed with dark thoughts".

This is the wealth of tax collectors, the foremen who become bosses and with a heavy hand rule over the farmhands, domineering over other people's wealth in a never-ending cascade of bills never paid and balance sheets never balanced. They often ended up usurping the property of rightful owners who were busy gambling at poker in private clubs or in their Palermo villas, far, far away from their landholdings and patrimonies, for which they had little interest to begin with. This was a spurious form of wealth, the archetype of a certain criminal economic and social class, which would continue, and still does, to do business with the butchers of Cosa Nostra, with the Mob's petty criminals, insuring privileges, as well as its own brand of law and order.

In light of this situation, and not only, Calò Montante's story is an exception to the rule. It's an exception because he chose to remain in Sicily without seeking Mafia favors. Because he believed in his own vision of industry, a high-tech industry by the standards of the times, that kept him from the blackmailing that took place on the fields of grain, and in the sulfur mines. He could have opted for managing the family patrimony and come to an understanding with the field hands and the foremen for the redistribution of sulfur or grain – one bundle for you, one for me. But, luckily, Calò had a different dream. He dreamed of achieving what Binda had achieved. He dreamed of a bicycle. A bicycle that didn't exist.

Two Wheels for Flying

There was already someone in Italy who had been making bicycles; for over thirty years. Edoardo Bianchi opened his first shop on Via Nirone in Milan in 1885. His company helped organize the Giro d'Italia. His fame was international. Bianchi was called on by Queen Margaret of the House of Savoy, while she was on vacation in Monza, to have a custom-built bicycle made for her. Bianchi made her a light blue model, with ivory handlebars and a wooden basket lined with red velvet. It bore the Savoy coat of arms in gold on the frame, and weighed eleven kilos. From that moment on, Bianchi was considered an official supplier to the royal house, and orders poured in from France, Spain and Portugal. Following Bianchi's success, bicycle factories sprung up in many parts of Italy.

However, the first bicycle to be manufactured in Sicily, in 1927, bore the name *Cicli Montante*, had a Serradifalco license plate and was made in a blacksmith's shop. Calò, with his self-taught mechanical knowhow and his experience at the lathe, put together his first bicycle piece by piece. It was a racing bike, built to endure. In Serradifalco everyone watched in awe as the young rider and builder crossed Corso Torrearse, today Via Roma, and headed up towards the church. He would then enter Via Crucillà on his way to Santa Croce, on a bicycle he had made with his own hands. Some were encouraged enough to order a bike from him, and soon word got around. Then a number of people wanted his bikes. As a result, production went up and Calò began to build custom-made cycles the way a tailor custom makes suits. He had a good head for business and immediately thought of a trademark in brass. He designed it himself and had it manufactured in Milan. Every bike that came out of the shop had the name *Cicli Montante* on the frame. Calò made racing bikes, touring bikes, women's bikes, men's bikes, children's bikes, recreational bikes and work bikes. These were bicycles with wide tires, perfectly suited for the roads of the time, with their pebbles, rocks, stones, mud and holes. These were tires that defied puncturing, tires that could climb mountains.

Calò was young and modern-minded. Not only was he a refined technician, but he also had a certain inclination towards elegance. The photos of the period show him in a well-tailored double-breasted suit, with a starched collar and an ivory-handled walking cane. Calò was thinking big: if he had the bikes, he needed a racing team. He recruited the best young cyclists in the area and had woolen jerseys and shorts with the company name made for them: block letters for the adults and italics for the younger riders. The jerseys were a big hit in Serradifalco, with people going out of their way to get their hands on them. After Mass on Sunday, one could see men proudly strutting the streets with their Montante jerseys.

Calò soon came to have his own shop, on Via Dante, which eventually became a meeting point for all sports fans in town. Amid the rattle and clang of the hammers and tongs, Calò put together a strategy for the eight-man Montante racing team, which included a cousin of the same name who acted as trainer. It also employed a motorcycle for the outings. The team participated in provincial races, regional races, and interregional races, with some positive results. Yet Calò's greatest triumph was the woolen jersey and shorts with his name on them. The reason for this is little known. Those light ochre jerseys, with a red and blue band in the middle, and the shorts with the Montante name on them, came from a family-run shop in Caltanissetta. And in that family there was a small, dark-skinned girl named Maria.

"'Next stop Caltanissetta!...'. The conductor shouts the words as the train comes to a stop, after twenty minutes through a dry, mountainous, not very pretty terrain, in which one can see the plumes of smoke rising from the sulfur mines. The station is a decent looking building, and within seconds the train empties and the twenty or so travelers make their way towards the exit.

"A handsome boulevard leads up towards the city. The, let's say, panoramic aspect of city, seen on high from the station, leaves something to be desired, though it is enough to dismiss the low opinion one hears of this all too forgotten, though always gentle, Sicilian city from travelers, especially travelling salesmen.

"From the Piazza Duomo flow other streets, though not as beautiful as the one from the station. These streets are boisterously animated, and loud. The population spends two thirds of its time on the street: in doorways, on balconies, or leaning out of windows. There is nothing in Caltanissetta in terms of monuments or special characteristics that distinguishes it from most of the other small cities in the central part of Sicily. In Caltanissetta one notices only a greater sense of cleanliness, a greater attention paid to the construction of buildings, and a certain tendency to re-modernize itself, things that one doesn't find in many of the other populated provincial towns and cities here. And this, given the various crises that afflict both the city and its outlying areas, is no small compliment".

This was how Caltanissetta presented itself to the journalist Gustavo Chiesi in 1892, when he published his *Sicilia illustrata,* a travel diary of visits to the towns and cities of an island that had been annexed to Italy for thirty years, but was still unknown to many Italians, many of whom considered it either exotic or uncivil. Chiesi dedicated four pages to Caltanissetta, much less than he reserved for the temples of Agrigento or Syracuse. Chiesi was a republican and an international journalist, and his tendency towards chronicle and sociology allowed him to look beyond mere historical facts. Sent to Sicily by Napoleone Colajanni, Chiesi offered some astonishing statistics in his brief account: "According to the 1871 census, the province of Caltanissetta had a 91.66 illiteracy rate. This would decline in the following decade to 86.50, meaning 230,430 people – 109,899 men and 120,531 women, who could not read or write. These are figures that should make our statesmen and politicians blush with shame, and should fill with sadness and pain the souls of those who are conscious of their duty towards the public good".

When Calò arrived in Caltanissetta, things were not much different. It still had a bare bones, sleepy air to it, covered with dust and melancholy. But for someone who came from a small town like Serradifalco, it must have seemed lively, dynamic and fascinating. In the '30s, Calò often rode the twenty-two kilometers that separated his town from the provincial capital. He loved to walk along the boulevards, past the city hall, and into the main squares, full of cafés and social clubs. He made new friends and always had a good time when he went to Caltanissetta.

Calò's experience was quite different from that of a man from Catania, who in the midst of an ideological crisis that threw into question his early adherence to Fascism, chose Caltanissetta as a means of distancing himself from the regime's success in Rome. Vitaliano Brancati was already a successful writer when he went to Caltanissetta to teach high school. He stayed there from 1934 to 1937, and sent his work to Leo Longanesi, editor of the literary journal *Omnibus*. Brancati also set one of his most bitter and tormented stories, *La noia nel '937* (*The Boredom of '37*), in Caltanissetta. It tells the story of Domenico Vannantò, his political and cultural struggles, and his progressive disengagement from the Fascist regime. Vannantò would get bored, Brancati, writes, "going from an avid, raging state of boredom that would devour everything around him that he found hateful, to a muted, leaden state of boredom, in which everything that was vain and petulant would fade, like a shout in the fog, to a dark, lugubrious state of boredom that would blanket, in the mind of the castigator, all that was foolishly joyous". Vannantò was bothered by everyone and everything and, in particular, by himself. "He stopped in Caltanissetta", Brancati writes, "because he immediately understood that here boredom would reach heights that no other place had ever dreamed of reaching. The city of yellow stone perched on a miserable plain; the hotel looking out onto the station from which the small, tired trains would occasionally huff and puff away; doors closed just after twilight, at the foot of which were dogs that would roll and turn trying to bite their tails; the clouds that would swiftly sail by, blown by a relentless wind; the statue of the Redeemer at the top of a hill attracting the mournful gazes of prisoners locked in a livid tenement building; the luthier's shop in front of the old church; the soaked cape of the policeman in the fog at dawn; lawyers gesticulating in front of their building doors, while above them their shirts gesticulated on the laundry line drawn from balcony to balcony; the conferences on matters of empire, the Pauline Sisters... there was nothing lacking here to raise boredom to a point of exultance".

Was that really what Caltanissetta was like? Maybe it was, in Brancati's lucidly dark thoughts. Maybe it was, to the degree that many small provincial cities are on every continent and at every latitude. Yet in those same years, at the same school, there was a student from Racalmuto by the name of Leonardo Sciascia, and his memories of the city are slightly different. "Between 1935 and 1940, Caltanissetta was a small Athens", Sciascia wrote, "if for no other reason than that in that period of stupidiocracy - presided over by donkeys, as Benedetto Croce said, a young man could still meet teachers like Luca Pignato, and men like the Protestant poet Calogero Bonavia, Father Lamantia, Aurelio Navarria, Luigi Monaco and Giuseppe Granata. Though these names might not ring a bell today, they exerted a great influence on me and others of my generation". The intellectual ferment in Caltanissetta prompted the first wave of anti-fascism, and eventually led to the rebirth of democratic parties in Sicily after the Second World War.

Emanuele Macaluso, from Caltanissetta, was one of the founders of the Communist Party in Sicily and has long been an important figure of the Italian Left. In his book *50 anni nel Pci* (*Fifty Years in the Italian Communist Party*) he recounts that "[t]wo large cafés competed for a demanding clientele, and the barmen who made espresso were great artisans. I remember two barmen who were particularly in demand: Di Bartolo and Falzone. The middle class that frequented those cafés lived a life that was in dignified and miserable contradistinction to that of manual laborers. Nonetheless, there was a certain political and cultural ferment in this southern city, on the outskirts of the empire, and there were those who truly questioned their condition. Caltanissetta was a city that was searching for its own identity, its own social and political life. After the

Liberation, it was a city that was very active politically".

Calogero Montante was neither intellectually nor politically inclined. Having grown up under Fascism, he came of age in a bourgeois family of landowners who saw in Mussolini the guarantor of their class interests. For his entire life, Calò maintained a subtle diffidence towards the grandeur and squalor of politics, and towards the dreams and deeds of politicians.

Though it might not have been Athens, Calogero Montante had good reason to spend time in Caltanissetta. That was where twenty-year-old Maria Giarratana lived. The Giarratana family had always been in the textile business, though it could count some illustrious ancestors in its family tree. There was a saintly Capuchin monk in the 17th century who was twice graced by the appearance of the Archangel Michael. And a nun at the end of the 19th century who was the Mother Superior of the College of Saint Mary in Caltanissetta. On the lay side of the family there were military men and professionals.

From our modern viewpoint it is hard to imagine what the rhythms and rites of Calò and Maria's courtship were. We do know, however, that Calò first saw her at the finish line of a race, where Maria stood ready to cheer on the winners. We also know that Calò cut the ribbon at that finish line, winning the prize, and winning Maria's gaze. And, finally, we know that at some point thereafter, the two became engaged, and soon married.

Gardens, Citrus Groves and Dreams

Bicycles serve to cover distances. A bicycle pushes you to travel, to fly and to lose yourself. When you're on a bicycle your mind wanders. So, let's let our mind wander. "Palermo is beautiful. Let's make it more beautiful". After the Second World War, politicians like Salvo Lima and Vito Ciancimino liked to recite these lines while they sacked the Golden Conch, issued building permits and made builders rich, tore down Liberty-style villas, aided Mafia bosses, and left a permanent scar on the face of Palermo.

But at the end of the 1920s, Palermo was truly a beautiful city. The tract of Via Libertà, just past the Teatro Politeama, was lined with villas, citrus groves and luxurious residential homes. Maybe at that time Palermo knew true happiness, at least according to the chronicles of the time. One person was certainly happy, and that was a boy who lived on Via Libertà. He was ten years old when his father called to him: "Come outside, I want you to see something".

There, in front of the house, was a Montante bicycle, luminous and silvery as its metal frame reflected the sun. It had been bought at Artale, in Via Mariano Stabile. Mimì, as the boy was called, mounted the bike and rode off to explore. In front of his villa was a mysterious and promising gate that led to a citrus grove, the intense green of the leaves shading the red of the oranges. Mimì's first ride took him down the garden paths, through the heavy fragrance of orange, mandarin and lemon, where nondescript apartment blocks of cement and glass now stand.

Mimì's range of exploration now took on new dimensions, flaring out in the direction of friends and family. Off he went towards Villa Cuccia, where his Uncle Enrico, the future head of Mediobanca, lived. Then to Terre Rosse, the residence of the aristocratic and libertine brothers Raimondo and Galvan Lanza. Everyone wanted to ride Mimì's bike. "I was the most envied kid in the neighborhood", Mimì La Cavera says, searching his memory. "We would ride out to Villa Pottino, where the baron would play cards with us and, under the pretense of teaching us poker, would cheat us out of our shoes".

These are snapshots of a lost city. That Montante bicycle rode through history, and Mimì took it with him to Rome, during the Second World War, where he served in the demolition corps. He also rode it through the streets of Rome in the confusion and chaos that followed Armistice Day, on September 8, 1943. The Montante stayed with Mimì through his years of dedication to the industrialization of Sicily, during which he helped found the Sicilian Businessmen's Association, the first association of its kind in Italy. "That was when I was arguing with the state monopolies and with Enrico Mattei, because I believed in a Sicily in which a business like

Montante's could grow and thrive, a network of large and small local industries", La Cavera says, with a certain tone of bitterness. "But I lost", he adds, "because the politicians decided to throw in their lot with the big corporations, the cathedrals in the desert".

The bicycle was still there, though, even when Mimì married Eleonora Rossi Drago, the beguiling actress. Eleonora had an unusual, and nervous disposition, and inadvertently became the subject of gossip when, as legend has it, she snapped out of a devastating melancholy upon meeting this small, lively and elegant Sicilian entrepreneur. Mimì and Eleonora lived in a villa on the Tiberina, in the Colle Romano area of Rome, where they hosted friends and parties. The Montante, still in working order, would take Mimì's valet Gioacchino on the twenty-kilometer round trip between Colle Romano and Riano for supplies. Then one day in 1985 Gioacchino rode the bike into a ditch. He made it through with a few broken bones. Gioacchino recovered nicely, but there was no way to salvage the Montante.

For almost sixty years, that Montante bicycle followed Mimì La Cavera wherever he went. Perhaps it is no coincidence that now, at the age of 92, Mimì La Cavera is the honorary president of the Sicilian Confindustria, the confederation of industries, which counts among its members the grandson of Calogero Montante, and other businessmen intent on refusing any form of coexistence with the Mafia. A make of bicycle, but above all the dreams hatched while riding it, unite the youth of today and yesterday, who together paint a different future for Sicily. But that's another race, for another time.

The Giro Comes to Sicily

In 1929 Calò received notice of his call to military service. He was a law-abiding citizen, but he was also no fool. Quite the opposite. He played his cards right until, some months later, he managed to avoid service. Like many others, Calò was called on to serve in the Second World War. But now, in the springtime of 1930, Calogero Montante was looking forward to one thing, and one thing only: the Giro d'Italia, for the first time, was coming to Sicily. This was certainly an exceptional event. The Giro was slated to start from the Straits of Messina, with the first stage running from Messina to Catania. The second stage was to run from Catania to Palermo, with the third running along the northern coast of the island from Palermo to Messina. From there the race was headed towards the continent, to a finish in Milan. Calò Montante was excited at the idea of seeing the cyclists up close, studying their bikes, and cheering on his hero, Alfredo Binda.
Except that Binda was to sit out the Giro, much to Calò's disappointment. Having already won

four consecutive Giros, Binda scared everyone, organizers and riders alike. The organizers had convinced the great rider to recuse himself from the race, and offered him the kingly sum of 22,500 lire, more in fact than the winner's share. Binda stayed at home and enjoyed his most clamorous victory, the one that cost him the least in terms of sweat and blood.

Needless to say, Calò was disappointed. He had truly wanted to see his hero on the roads of Sicily. As it turned out, he had to content himself with the exploits of Luigi Marchisio, who won the third stage and went on to wear the pink jersey in Milan on June 8th, at the finish line. Calò consoled himself with Binda's autobiography, *Le mie vittorie e le mie sconfitte. Come si corre su strada. Consigli ai giovani (My Victories and My Defeats: How to Ride the Roads, My Advice to Young Riders)*, published in 1931 by the *Stabilimento Tipografico Littorio di Varese*. It was a book that always had a place on Calò's bookshelf. But Calogero Montante consoled himself primarily with the small successes he experienced racing with his Montante Team. He cut quite a decent figure as a rider in regional and interregional races, taking his racing team all over southern Italy.

At the same time, there were more pressing matters at hand. Calò's marriage to Maria, for example, which took place on April 28, 1934 in Caltanissetta. The photographs of the time reveal a twenty-five-year-old Calò, dressed in a dark, tailored suit, with a white bowtie and kerchief in his breast pocket. Maria, then twenty-two, was dressed in a white wedding gown of French cut, with a short veil and a handful of gladiolas. They seem serious in the studio shots, though they were probably just nervous. As expected, their first son, Luigi, was born a year later, to be followed by Francesco and Gaetana, who everyone called Nuccia.

The Army Rides Montante

One is still young at twenty-seven, though in 1935 a twenty-seven-year-old was considered an adult. Calò at that age was a businessman, an athlete and a father. Marriage had made him an even more reserved man, and the time he spent out of the shop he spent at home with his family. He was never one for the daily *passeggiata* along the main street of town, a social event pregnant with gossip and backstabbing. Nor one for the wicker chairs of the local social club, where the men of the town, grouped by age or job, would pass summer nights observing the *passeggiata* of well-dressed families and offer their own takes on the standard local small-talk and scandals, already known to all. In southern Italian towns and cities there are social clubs for everyone: veterans of war, artisans, workers' cooperatives, miners and salt workers. Reigning above these social clubs are the gentlemen's clubs, the casinos of civilized men, where landowners and noblemen sit at the green felt tables to feel the ultimate thrill of throwing away their last piece of land on the turn of a card. Sicilian literature is full of social club conversation, on the subject of politics or women. Women of the imagination or of dreams; fantasy women who could be insulted in a fit of "gallantry". In Sicily there are men, as Brancati pointed out, who have left nothing to posterity but the impression of their posteriors on the armchairs of the local social club.

Calò Montante, however, was a different race of man. A man who never liked to hide behind words. Though he spent his most of his life between shop and home, he did love the weekend picnic with family and close friends. Calò would arrive on his Montante, and heaven forbid if someone showed up on a Bianchi or Legnano. In those cases, Calò would explode, go off on a rant and eventually leave the party. In these cases, his wife Maria was the only one who could placate him. She was a strong women, able to raise a family, take care of household affairs and become, as some Sicilian women are, the arbiters of their husbands' and children's destiny. If it's true that there is a distinctive Sicilian form of matriarchy, then this was it, particularly in the 1930s. This idea was based, and still is, on the notion that men rule and women decide. That seems to fit Maria Giarratana Montante to a tee. For his entire life, Calò Montante found in Maria his ally, his accomplice, and his supporter in times of difficulty.

Yet Calò was not the type to have his head in the sand. He travelled all over Italy on business, often visiting Milan and Turin to contact the company that made headlights, and the dynamos that powered them. He travelled all over Italy selling his bicycles and looking for retailers, given that the Sicilian market wasn't enough to ensure his success. At one point he became the official supplier of bicycles for the Italian military police – the Carabinieri, and the Department of Public Safety. For the Carabinieri, Montante built two models of bicycle: the Trooper's Model and the Officer's Model. The Trooper's model had a folding frame that supported front and rear baskets, pneumatic tires, mudguards, and front and rear brakes. It weighed sixteen kilos. From old yellowed papers found in the Montante archives there are handwritten letters from Calò to the Office of the Carabinieri stating that the Trooper's model cost 470 lire. The Officer's model cost 510 lire, and had a different finish on the frame, though the real difference was in the tires. The Officer's model had solid tires. This may seem strange when one considers that solid tires added to the weight of the bicycle and made it more difficult to maneuver, though the reason for this lies in what was, at the time, a sense of decorum. Pneumatic tires were subject to flats. What would it have looked like to see a Carabiniere officer, elegantly dressed in his uniform, bent down in the mud to change a flat tire? As a result, the officer's corps of the Italian state police, accustomed as they were to taking orders without asking why, were forced to work harder than the troopers under their command.

What emerges from the time, as though through a wide-angle lens, are images that seem to come from the first page of the *Domenica del Corriere*, the Italian equivalent of the *Saturday Evening Post*. The carabiniere on his bike, with his cape, captured in a Norman Rockwell-like sketch by Achille Beltrame, an image that would adorn many an Italian home. This image even survives today on the Carabiniere calendar.

In the 1930s, Montante made all sorts of bicycles for all sorts of needs, as the advertisements of the time claimed. There were classic touring bikes, with dynamos, and front and rear lights, and accessories, that sold for between 380 and 400 lire. There were racing bikes that sold for 780 lire. And then there were custom-made bikes with super accessories, work bikes and "Little Prince" tricycles that cost over 1,000 lire. One thousand lire was not a negligible sum in those days. A kilo of bread cost 1.60 lire; a kilo of potatoes cost 50 lire. A skilled laborer earned 400 lire a month, and in 1939 Umberto Melnati sang: "If I could earn a thousand lire a month, without exaggerating, I would be sure to find happiness / A humble job, I couldn't ask for more / All I want to do is work to have an easy life". The film *Mille lire al mese* (*A Thousand Lire a Month*) was inspired by this song, and was a big hit, with theaters full of people enjoying the romance between Melnati and the beautiful 18-year-old actress Alida Valli. A thousand lire a month, at the time, was the salary of a company manager. Though today it corresponds to a mere € 800, in the 1930s you could more than have got by on that. Indeed, you could probably have afforded a Montante bicycle.

The World Is Changing

Foul winds were blowing. Blowing from Berlin and from Rome. The world was roaring and its echoes could be heard all the way down in Serradifalco. Like all Italians, Calò heard Mussolini's June 10, 1940 speech on the radio, a speech given from Piazza Venezia, in Rome. "A time tinged by destiny now crosses the sky of our homeland. A time of irrevocable decisions. The declaration of war has already been given to the ambassadors of Great Britain and France...". In the deafening roar of applause we don't know if Calò felt the same wave of excitement that so many Italians felt as they faced a war that they thought would be short and sweet, but turned out to be long and lost. Mussolini, with his words, was playing with his own destiny, that of Italy, and that of Calò. Calò was thirty-five years old, had three children and a successful business, but his country was calling him to arms. He was called to the front when Italy was on its last legs, when defeat was almost certain. In 1943, Calogero Montante, in uniform, left for the Yugoslavian front. He was there on September 8 of that year, when the armistice, and the definitive decline of the Italian empire, was signed. *Tutti a casa* (*Everybody Go Home*), as Luigi Comencini would say years later in his film with Alberto Sordi and Eduardo De Filippo, a comment on those tumultuous, confusing days. Except that Calò Montante's journey home was delayed. He was taken prisoner, first by the Germans (who had become enemy combatants), and then by Tito's army.

As the crossing of stars goes, we should here note a particularly interesting, fundamental one. Montante was in Yugoslavia in 1943, when the Allied troops were landing in Sicily. He had no way of knowing that a seventeen-year-old from Porto Empedocle was taking refuge with his family in a house in Serradifalco. He had no way of knowing that that young man would mount a Montante bicycle on a July day on a ride towards Agrigento to find out what had happened to his father and the family home. And furthermore, he had no way of knowing that years later that young man would become a writer and would recount his journey, through a Sicily populated by American soldiers, on a bicycle made by Calò himself. Yet perhaps it is the missed appointments with destiny that mark the mysterious coincidences of our lives. And if today we recount the story of Calò as if it were a Sicilian fable, we owe much to a bicycle that linked the lives of two men who never met.

The Bicycle Is Dead, Long Live the Bicycle

Calò's return to Serradifalco after the Second World War was much like his father's return to the town after the First World War. But this is the shared story of all survivors of war. Even now, in the 1940s, Serradifalco was impoverished, though it hadn't taken any direct hits. In Sicily, the war had ended two years before it had in the rest of Italy. It ended when the first jeeps full of American soldiers handing out chewing gum and Camel cigarettes made their way through Serradifalco. In that small town in central Sicily, there was no resistance, no civil war. There were no partisan fighters, or late reprisals. The remnants of the war were signs of a new poverty, of new needs.

In the evening, the main streets and piazzas of Serradifalco were full of people. People talking. Talking a lot. As Angelo Petyx remembers, "On Saturday night, especially in spring and summer, the piazza of my town was an anthill of human activity. It was beautiful piazza... and so people really loved to take the *passeggiata* and exchange a few words. This was a town of politicos, people who got hot under the collar in a hurry. People who couldn't see straight because of an innocuous word or two, because they were so self conscious of their poverty with respect to other more socially and politically advanced regions of Italy". "A town of politicos", Petyx says. What he means, I think, is a certain passion for civic life, a gusto for polemics, one-liners, cutting nicknames, strident insults. In the years after World War II, politics were the new passion. For some it meant civic engagement, for others juicy business deals.

Perhaps it was Calò's natural diffidence that kept him from politics. He ploughed all of his energy into his work. Having traveled outside of Sicily, Calò was convinced that the bicycle was destined to become obsolete. People with money were buying motorcycles, trucks, sidecars, automobiles. Bicycles were for poor folk.

Poor folk like Antonio Ricci, the Roman worker of Vittorio De Sica's *Ladri di biciclette* (*Bicycle Thieves*). In 1948, De Sica's film became a worldwide manifesto of Italian cinematic neorealism. It was the simple, dramatic, and highly symbolic story of a man desperately looking for his bicycle. A bicycle, a thing of little worth for the viewer, the police and, indeed, the world, is of vital importance for the poor wretch who has nothing else. Antonio Ricci's bicycle looks like a Montante: the same model, the same build. In fact, Calogero Montante had sold fifteen bicycles to the Cinecittà film studios in 1946. Who knows, maybe that was a Montante in De Sica's Oscar-winning film.

Calò began reconverting his business. In addition to selling and renting bikes, he began selling motorcycles: Lambrettas, Rumis, Mas, Cimattis, BMs, Mivals, Guzzis, Aprilias and Ducatis began lining the street in front of his shop on Corso Garibaldi, under the jealous gaze of teenagers and adults alike. Calò was proud of his goods, roaring the motor and showing off the streamlined design of his motorcycles for all. Yet in his soul he still harbored a love for bicycles, and racing, and the Giro. The Giro offered new rivalries, like the one between Coppi and Bartali. Italy at that time was divided by sports and by politics. There was the Christian Democratic Party and the Communist Party, Peppone and don Camillo, Fausto and Gino. Coppi was the high symbol of lay Italy, while Bartali was the emblem of traditional Catholicism. In 1948, Calogero Montante decided to back Bartali, and that year's Giro was destined to become a symbol of the age. Some even claimed that the rivalry race between Coppi and Bartali engaged the Italians so much that it cooled the escalating tensions in a country split between allegiances to the Christian Democrats and to the Communists, a situation that ended in an electoral victory of the Christian Democrats on April 18.

The next year, Mario Ferretti's radio account of Coppi's 192-kilometer break-away in the '49 Giro entered into the annals of legend. "There's just one rider in command. His jersey is light blue. His name is Fausto Coppi".

With Coppi and Bartali's duel, Italy seemed to be making its way up from the low points of the Second World War. Their rivalry gradually evolved into friendship, and there is a photo in which Coppi and Bartali exchange a bottle of water while racing. Neither of the two would ever say which one initiated the exchange. Legend achieves its status through omission. From north to south, Italians turned on their televisions and saw Coppi and Bartali: on Mario Riva's *Il musichiere*, Mike Bongiorno's game show, and Sergio Zavoli's *Processo alla tappa*. In television, cycling found its ideal format for narration and glorification. In those crude black and white images, every wrinkle of effort, every drop of sweat, and every gesture of joy and sadness was exalted.

A Man of Few Words

Calò was not one to joke around. He had been born and raised in central Sicily, an arid land. "I believe that no Sicilian is more dignified, more constant, more thoughtful, more full of pride and pain than the Sicilian from the sulfur lands", the writer Vincenzo Consolo once said. "It is as if, divested of all illusions, he has seen, once and for all, the raw truth of existence and, having accepted it, defends himself solely with intelligence and bitter irony".

Calò loved his family. It was an ancient and in-grained form of respect. He was a man of his times, brought up in a certain way. "He was very close to my mother", Calò's son Luigi says. "He would leave home and go to work, and then leave work and come home. There were no distractions. We would all have lunch together every day. On Sundays, we would go to church together, and then take the Fiat 600 and go for a picnic in the country".

Calò was not a sensitive father. In a certain sense he was an authoritarian figure, particularly at work, where he taught his sons the tricks of the trade and then expected the most from them. They were to be an example to the other workers. As sons of the owner, they had to work harder, earn their daily bread with more sweat. Those were difficult years: the shop sold and repaired motorcycles, worked on engines, modified body parts on the lathe, and built new ones. Everything was done by hand. "We worked day and night", Luigi says.

Calò was always in the shop, elegant and seemingly impermeable to oil, gas and grease. "I don't know how he did it", Luigi says, "but he was always clean as a whistle. Immaculate". He also always had something to say. It was never easy to convince Calò that there might be different ways of doing things, which naturally caused some friction when his sons became adults and wanted to decide things for themselves. On the other hand, he was generous. His sons always had the newest, shiniest motorcycles. They were the most envied kids on the block.

There was only one person who could ever make Calò change his mind, and that was his wife, Maria. This was no easy task; one needed "the touch", as they say in Sicilian, the knowledgeable art of bending a husband's will without hurting or humiliating him, and even, in the process, of exalting him in the eyes of the family. Calò could be hardheaded, and had been since he was young, when some family members would arrive at a picnic on a bicycle that hadn't come from his hands. Then, he would fly off the handle, abandon the family outing and wander off until he had blown off enough steam. Later in life, if he was contradicted he would close himself off in silence. This was typical of a man from this part of Sicily. "I believe in the Sicilian of few words", Leonardo Sciascia once wrote, "in the Sicilian who doesn't get upset. In the Sicilian who buries everything inside and suffers".

The Province of the Three Bosses

Sicily has a double geography. The official one divides the island into nine provinces and three hundred and ninety towns. The other one doesn't appear on any road map or in any school book.

That is the geography of the "families" and "territories". It's a criminal geography that has been mapped only by the police. This map is not public, though everyone has memorized it, because memorizing it is often a matter of life or death.

Everyone in Sicily knew, for example, that on the morning of July 14, 1943 an American fighter plane flew low over Villalba, in the province of Caltanissetta, thirty-five kilometers north of Serradifalco. The Allied troops had landed on the beaches between Licata and Syracuse just four days earlier, following brief skirmishes. They were now set to advance towards the interior. Everyone said that the plane had flown for some time above Villalba, with a yellow flag blowing behind on the tail wing. When it was perpendicular to the bell tower of the church, a package was dropped. It was promptly picked up and delivered to its addressee, Don Calogero Vizzini. The package contained a yellow scarf with a black "L" stitched onto it, the L referring to Lucky Luciano, the powerful American mobster. Many say that days later, Calò Vizzini sent a coded message to another local Mafia boss, Giuseppe Genco Russo. Everyone claims that the message was that Cosa Nostra was giving the green light to the American troops to advance on the island without interference, and telling the Yanks that they could count on local Mob bosses for support.

Everyone knew this story, which was discussed in hushed tones in local piazzas. Everyone was sure that this was how things had gone, and many even believe so today, despite the fact that a number of esteemed historians have refuted the story. However, this is such an interesting anecdote that even John Dickie, the English historian, recounted it in his 2005 book *Cosa Nostra*, if only to go on to confute it. But, true or not, it certainly illustrates how much influence was attributed to Don Calogero Vizzini and the Mafia of the province of Caltanissetta, who were deemed capable of secretly handling Operation Husky, the biggest military maneuver ever carried out on Sicilian soil.

If, in the immediate post-war era, Palermo was the sun of the Sicilian Mafia constellation, and Corleone was its rising star, the province of Caltanissetta contained the planets that constituted the entire system. Three towns, three names, three bosses. There was Calò Vizzini in Villalba, Giuseppe Genco Russo in Mussomeli, and Giuseppe Di Cristina in Riesi. If one were to draw lines between these towns, Serradifalco would appear almost at the center, closed in by three Mafia bosses. They were all different, but had in common the prestige of being both inside and outside the Mafia. Officially these three mobsters were nothing but semiliterate peasants, though ruthless and influential enough to keep most of Sicily in a tight grip. Their spider's web included almost every business deal and economic interest: mining, public bids, university exams, and election results, to mention just a few. Calagero Vizzini, who had shut down a campaign speech by communist candidates Girolamo Li Causi and Emanuele Macaluso in the town square of Villalba, setting off bombs and shots, had this to say in a 1954 interview with Italian journalist Indro Montanelli: "In every society there has to be a category of person who sets things right when things get complicated. Usually this falls to state functionaries. But where the state is absent or doesn't have sufficient powers, there are private citizens ..." Vizzini concluded by saying, "The Mafia? Does the Mafia even exist?".

Here is Genco Russo, interviewed by Leonardo Sciascia in 1965: "So, you're from Racalmuto. So, tomorrow, let's say, I've got to take care of some bureaucratic matter in Racalmuto, and you're there. I come to see you, and you help me as much as you can to take care of that matter. Then one day you've got something to take care of in Mussomeli, and you come find me. I'm at your disposal. We've become friends, no? That's it. You can say it's Mafia, or it's not Mafia, I don't know... I call it friendship. People who meet each other, take to each other, help each other. There's an argument: let's step in and help resolve it. Someone needs help: let's give help. If you want to call that Mafia, then I'm a Mafioso. The truth is that no one, up to now, understands anything of all this".

Giuseppe Di Cristina, the "tiger of Riesi", was the only one of the big three not to die of natural causes. He was killed by Luciano Liggio and Totò Riina of the Corleonese family in 1978. One could say that he was the least loquacious of the Big Three. He seemed to prefer the gun to the word. He was at the command of an operation on October 28, 1979, when mobsters dressed as physicians made their way into Palermo's Civico Hospital and killed the hotel owner Candido Ciuni, who had been injured some days before in an assassination attempt. Towards the end, Di Cristina was shocked and scared by the rise of the Corleonese and tried to pass on information to the police that would help thwart their ascendancy. The Corleonese killed him before he could reveal everything.

This book wasn't meant as a history of the Caltanissetta Mafia, and doesn't want to become one. Yet it's important to understand that in post-war Sicily, living and working in a town like Serradifalco meant running up against certain types of men, certain types of mindsets, and certain types of crimes. It may be that the Mafia wasn't interested in a bicycle maker. They probably had bigger fish to fry: other, more lucrative businesses, such as real-estate, regional organizations, large industrial plants and building speculation. And land interests, in which the Caltanissetta Mafia had its roots.

But what is important to see in Calogero Montante is the fact that he was a businessman in a very difficult time, and despite that fact he never sought help from the many Mafia bosses that populated the evening *passeggiata* in town squares. What should be pointed out is that Calò never let himself be taken in by what Sicilians call the *annacata*, the *strut*, of the local Mob bosses. Calò preferred to stay away from that sort of thing, and when some local somebody let him know that he expected a free bike, Calò pretended that he didn't know what the man was talking about, and rang up the sale as if nothing were amiss. It may not seem like much, but for that time - and indeed for our own - it was something.

A Gentleman of a Bygone Time

Calò Montante could never imagine life without work. He could never abide by the idea of living off someone else's labors. His life as a businessman had taught him that everything has a cost, a price. This is the same kind of mentality that, fifty years later, would lead another Sicilian businessman, Libero Grassi, to his death. Grassi's was not a heroic death. There was no inclination towards martyrdom, as some fellow businessman indecorously suggested after his assassination. Grassi's gesture was pure heresy in a city where everyone paid extortion and kept quiet about it. It was a well argued and intellectually sound heresy, as one could gather from the various television interviews that he gave. "I will never pay protection money to the Mafia", Grassi repeated to journalists, "because I have been in business forty years, and I know that a businessman does not entrust his assets to others. I'm not a particularly courageous man, just someone who wants to defend his interests. Paying protection money is stupid. You pay them and then they're back again asking for more. At that point, it makes more sense to go to the police". But when Libero Grassi went to the police, he was alone, isolated. He was killed by Mafia hit men on a late August morning in 1991. Day after day from the 1950s on, in line with Grassi's work ethic, Calò Montante would don a jacket and tie and go to work at his shop. He also devoured sports magazines, newspapers and, indeed, any sort of reading material he could get his hands on, even if his eyesight was progressively failing him. Behind his back, people in town accused him of being stingy, a judgment that his great granddaughter Alessandra vehemently denies. "They say that he was a little too attached to his possessions, though for someone like him, who had lived through good times and bad, not personal or family matters, but within the context of a historical epoch, that would seem perfectly logical", she says. "My great grandfather was a wonderful man, and was admired by everyone. I feel proud to be able to speak well of him, to remember the key episodes of his life, and to thank him for having laid the foundation for our family business, which now operates solidly within the market, and offers us our daily bread after seventy years of work and experience through three generations".

Unfortunately, these are words that Calò was not there to hear. They were spoken at his funeral at the church of Serradifalco on the afternoon of June 15, 2000. Calogero Montante managed to see the new millennium, but died shortly thereafter at the age of 92. At his funeral, in the crowded church, his young great granddaughter asked to speak at the microphone. With a voice breaking with emotion, she had this to say: "I want to talk about my great grandfather Calogero, the founder of the Montante Company. I want to talk about him not only for this reason or because he was my great grandfather. I want to talk about him because he was an extraordinary person, a person who was, and will always be, special for us. My great grandfather always distinguished himself in character and personality. He was a gentleman of a bygone time, though always thoroughly modern: a bit volatile, strong-willed, indomitable, and maybe a little hard-going at times, and this may have made him difficult to understand. But he was, as they say, all of a piece: he was rigorous, intransigent and inflexible. The fact is, that you had to do things his way or no way. End of story".

End of story. Until his dying day, his descendants consulted him on all sorts of business matters. The Montante Company has changed a great deal since 1946. It has gone from making bicycles to selling motorcycles, and then, gradually, to producing shock absorbers for industrial vehicles. It has grown, enlarged and become stronger. But this is another chapter, a chapter that would take us outside the story at hand.

This story began with a legend. Just before midnight, a boy climbed up onto the Testa dell'Acqua Fountain dreaming of being part of an enchanted fair, during which he would buy the golden fruit. This is a real and entirely possible story, even in Sicily. Calò Montante had no contact with writers or noblemen, though he could have explained to Tomasi di Lampedusa, the author of *Il Gattopardo (The Leopard)*, that even in Serradifalco the "sins of the father" don't always fall to the sons. This is a simple story, with little adventure or heroism. It is simply the story of a man who wanted to ride a bike.

Rome, february 2008

Photos

1. Calogero Montante, 1931.

2. A postcard of Corso Torrearse, in Serradifalco, 1926.

3. A postcard of Corso Garibaldi, in Serradifalco, 1926.

4. Calogero Montante lifting one of his bicycles to demonstra-
te, what was for the time, its extraordinary lightness. The
bicycle was a CPN Model *Cambio leva Margherita* from 1928.

5. Calogero Montante during a 1928 race, rotating the wheel to achieve change of speed.

6. Calogero Montante and his racing team during a pause in
their training routines, 1929.

7. Calogero Montante, center, with his new model of racing bike. On the left is his cousin and namesake, who was the team's trainer, 1928.

8. The Montante team jersey.

9. The Montante Bicycle Shop on Via Dante, in Serradifalco, *circa* 1932. On the right is Elena, one of the first workers at the shop.

10. A carabiniere officer on a Montante bicycle, 1932.

═CICLI═
MONTANTE

MODELLO MILITARE

FORNITO
ALLA REALE
ARMA
DEI CARABINIERI

Modello tutto verniciato in colore grigio/nero con porta spallacci, porta mantellina, porta fucile, gomme piene Pirelli, raggi rinforzati di mm. $2\frac{1}{2}$, doppio freno a leve esposte, ruota libera, parafanghi SAF, sella speciale elastica, borsetta con accessori e campanello.

L. 530

SOLIDITÀ

SCORREVOLEZZA

SICUREZZA
E
AFFIDABILITÀ
GARANTITE

SERRADIFALCO

11. A Montante price list.

12. A Montante price list.

13. A Montante price list.

14. Calogero Montante and Maria Giarratana on their wedding day, 1934.

15. Calogero Montante in Serradifalco, 1929.

16. Calogero Montante's son, Luigi, in Via Dante, Serradi-falco, 1938.

17. Calogero Montante's daughter, Nuccia, 1944.

18. The Montante and Giarratana families on a country outing in Contrada Niscima, in Caltanissetta. Calogero Montante is seated second to left. Standing behind him is his wife, Maria Giarratana, holding their son, Luigi, 1935.

19. Group photo of the Montante and Giarratana cousins, *circa* 1939.

20. Maria Giarratana Montante, 1938.

21. Calogero Montante's sons, Luigi and Francesco, in a photograph from the Camilleri Studio in Caltanissetta, 1941. The tricycle was a Montante.

22. Mimì La Cavera on a Montante bicycle, Rome, 1939.

Bibliography and Sources

I am indebted to many authors for their invaluable contributions to this book. I owe a particular debt of gratitude to Felice Dell'Utri, whose research of original documents was the architectonic structure on which I built Calò's story.

Sebastiano Aglianò, *Che cos'è questa Sicilia*, Sellerio, Palermo, 1996.

Alfredo Binda, *Le mie vittorie e le mie sconfitte*, Stabilimento Tipografico Littorio, Varese, 1931.

Giorgio Boatti, Bolidi, *Quando gli italiani incontrarono le prime automobili*, Mondadori, Milano, 2006.

Vitaliano Brancati, *La noia nel '937*, in *Racconti, teatro, scritti giornalistici*, Mondadori, Milano, 2003.

Michele Bruccheri, *Ritratti serradifalchesi*, supplement of the periodical *La voce del nisseno*, Serradifalco, March, 2005, April 2006, August 2007.

Alfio Caruso, *Da cosa nasce cosa. Storia della mafia dal 1943 ad oggi*, Longanesi, Milano, 2005.

Gustavo Chiesi, *La Sicilia illustrata*, Vito Cavallotti Editore, Palermo, 1980.

Vincenzo Consolo, *Di qua dal faro,* Mondadori, Milano, 1999.

Felice Dell'Utri, *Calogero Montante.* Serradifalco 1908-2000, manuscript in the Montante Family Archives.

John Dickie, *Cosa Nostra*, Laterza, Roma-Bari, 2005.

Louise Hamilton Caico, *Vicende e costumi siciliani*, Lussografica, Caltanissetta, 2006.

Salvatore Lupo, *Storia della mafia. Dalle origini ai nostri giorni*, Donzelli, Roma, 2004.

Emanuele Macaluso, *50 anni nel Pci*, Rubbettino, Soveria Mannelli, 2003.

Indro Montanelli, *Gli incontri*, Rizzoli, Milano, 1973.

Angelo Petyx, *La miniera occupata*, Salvatore Sciascia editore, Caltanissetta-Roma, 2002.

Gaetano Savatteri, *I siciliani*, Laterza, Bari, 2005.

Leonardo Sciascia, *Il padrino e il professore*, in *Malgrado tutto. Periodico cittadino di commento e cultura*, Racalmuto, December 2007, previously published in *Mondo Nuovo*, June 1965.

Leonardo Sciascia, *Le parrocchie di Regalpetra*, in *Opere 1956-1971*, Bompiani, Milano, 1987.

Leonardo Sciascia, Marcelle Padovani, *La Sicilia come metafora*, Mondadori, Milano, 1979.

Giuseppe Tomasi di Lampedusa, *Il Gattopardo*, Feltrinelli, Milano, 1958 edition.

Marco Ventura, *Il campione e il bandito*, Il Saggiatore, Milano, 2006.

Storie del Giro e dell'Italia, www.gazzetta.it/ Speciali/Giroditalia

Printed and bound by Leva Arti Grafiche s.p.a.
Sesto S. Giovanni (MI)